THE LOLLIPOP MONSTER

ERIC T. KRACKOW

Schiffer Publishing Ltd

4880 Lower Valley Road · Atglen, Pennsylvania 19310

Schiffer Books are available at special discounts for bulk purchases for sales promotions or premiums. Special editions, including personalized covers, corporate imprints, and excerpts can be created in large quantities for special needs. For more information contact the publisher:

Published by Schiffer Publishing Ltd.
4880 Lower Valley Road
Atglen, PA 19310
Phone: (610) 593-1777; Fax: (610) 593-2002
E-mail: Info@schifferbooks.com

For the largest selection of fine reference books on this and related subjects, please visit our web site at **www.schifferbooks.com**
We are always looking for people to write books on new and related subjects. If you have an idea for a book please contact us at the above address.

This book may be purchased from the publisher.
Include $5.00 for shipping.
Please try your bookstore first.
You may write for a free catalog.

In Europe, Schiffer books are distributed by
Bushwood Books
6 Marksbury Ave.
Kew Gardens
Surrey TW9 4JF England
Phone: 44 (0) 20 8392 8585; Fax: 44 (0) 20 8392 9876
E-mail: info@bushwoodbooks.co.uk
Website: www.bushwoodbooks.co.uk

Copyright © 2011 by Eric T. Krackow

Library of Congress Control Number: 2010941408

ISBN: 978-0-7643-3773-4
Printed in China

This book is dedicated to my father, Arnold. Love you Dad.

Special thanks to my wife Heather for all her help and hard work. Thank you, sweetheart.

The land of Monstoria is a most unusual place. The beautiful sky rises above the sleepy mountains in the distance, its purple clouds swirling together in a remarkable way. The vast horizon is lined from end to end with trees stretched out one after the other.

But the most amazing things of all, in this strange and special place, are the monsters who live among its mountains and its trees. There are hundreds of them, and each one is more spectacular than the next. Some are large, some are small, and some are in between. Some have scales, some have fur, and some are covered in plaid. Some have two eyes, others have four, and some have only one! And they all live together in the wonderful land of Monstoria.

One of the Monstoria monsters is a curious creature named "Larry," who lives deep in the woods. He is a huge monster with pink fur marked with purple stripes. He has a long trunk for a nose and two long horns that grow from his head. A row of large purple scales runs down his back, from the top of his neck to the tip of his tail. You can always tell it's Larry, because, wherever he goes, he always carries a large sack of lollipops with him. He absolutely loves his lollipops and is always happy to share them with his friends.

While Larry may look strange to you and me, in Monstoria everyone would look strange to us, but not to each other. What makes Larry different from the other large monsters who live there is that Larry wasn't mean or bad, not in any way. You see, if you are a big monster in Monstoria, you are expected to pick on monsters who are smaller than you. It is just part of being huge. But Larry doesn't think that is right.

Call it a feeling or a hunch, but Larry knows deep in his heart that all creatures are special and that you shouldn't be mean to other monsters just because they are different. He believes that being kind to others is the best way to be. But it isn't always easy being kind, and, in Monstoria, for a very long time Larry wasn't liked by the other big monsters because of it.

Then, not too long ago, Larry was walking down the forest path when he saw something that changed his life in Monstoria forever. On a hilltop not far from him, three big monsters had surrounded three little monsters. They were not being very nice.

"Hey, stop that!" cried the small, furry, blue monster named Zabby. "That's not yours, give it back!" The big monsters had taken Zabby's toy and were tossing it back and forth, while they laughed at her. "This is our toy now," they taunted.

One of them held the toy high above Zabby's head. This was Jagger, the leader of the group of big monsters. He was a large, orange monster who often picked on smaller monsters like Zabby. "I'm bigger than you and there's nothing you can do about it!" Jagger teased.

There was nothing else they could do. Zabby and her friends, Xue and Xola, lowered their monster heads and slowly walked away from Jagger and his mean buddies. The big monsters laughed and pointed at them as they walked away. Zabby was a very sad little monster.

While this was going on, Larry stood with his lollipop in his mouth and watched what the big monsters did to the little monsters. Finally he decided he must do something about it. "Um, excuse me?" Larry said softly, because he was a little scared. "Does that toy belong to you?"

"It does now." Jagger laughed. "I just took it from that puny little monster over there! Do you want to play with it?"

"But that toy doesn't belong to you...you should give it back to Zabby." Larry's voice was getting a little stronger. Zabby and her friends heard the commotion and turned to watch.

Jagger's grin slowly vanished from his face and he moved toward Larry. You could see in his eyes that he was angry. "So what are you gonna do about it, Larry?" Jagger demanded.

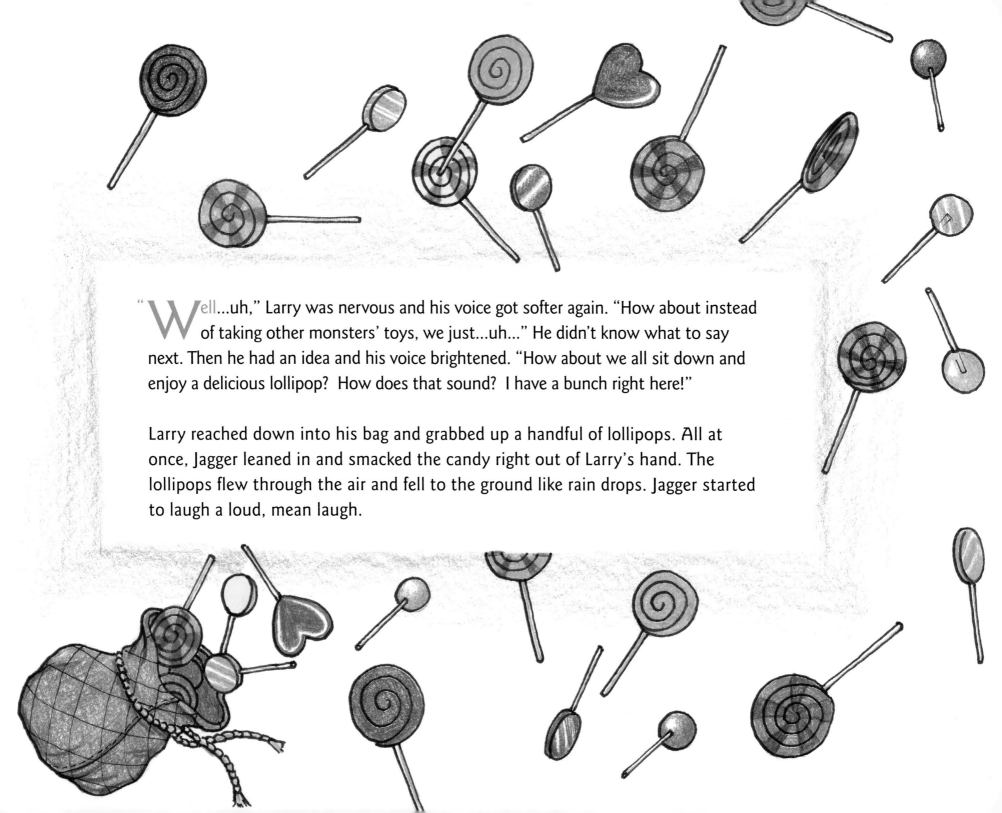

"Well...uh," Larry was nervous and his voice got softer again. "How about instead of taking other monsters' toys, we just...uh..." He didn't know what to say next. Then he had an idea and his voice brightened. "How about we all sit down and enjoy a delicious lollipop? How does that sound? I have a bunch right here!"

Larry reached down into his bag and grabbed up a handful of lollipops. All at once, Jagger leaned in and smacked the candy right out of Larry's hand. The lollipops flew through the air and fell to the ground like rain drops. Jagger started to laugh a loud, mean laugh.

The mean monsters turned around and began to walk away, making fun of Larry as they went. Then, Jagger turned to him and said "Hey, 'Larry the Loser!' catch!" He threw Zabby's toy at Larry and it landed right in front of him. He slumped down to his knees and slowly picked up his lollipops and the toy.

After the mean monsters were gone, Zabby and her friends peeked around the tree and began to inch closer to Larry. "Thanks for sticking up for us, Larry. That was really nice, what you did." Larry tried his hardest to put a smile on his face. "Think nothing of it," he said. "Just because they're bigger than you, doesn't mean they should be mean to you. I know that I wouldn't want someone to be mean to me." He handed the toy back to Zabby and began walking home to the woods. He was very sad.

Word about what Larry had done spread quickly through Monstoria and the big monsters began treating him worse than ever. Wherever Larry went, they ignored him and turned their heads away from him. Sometimes he could hear them whisper "There goes Larry the Loser" as he passed by. Larry became so upset that he didn't even want to eat lollipops anymore.

Larry knew he had done the right thing sticking up for the smaller monsters, but that didn't make him feel any better. He never understood why big monsters picked on little monsters, but he knew it was wrong. Unfortunately, the other monsters didn't see it that way, and it seemed like none of them would talk to him ever again.

One day, Larry was sitting on a large green rock at the edge of the forest, thinking about the way things had turned out. Jagger and his friends spotted Larry there and went over to give him some more trouble.

"What's going on, Larry the Loser? Why aren't you out with your little monster friends?" Jagger asked Larry, while the other monsters stood by and laughed. Larry tried his best to ignore him, but Jagger would not stop teasing him.

"Ooooh wook at me," Jagger started to say in a cruel, mocking way. "I'm Warry the woser and I'm not mean to wittle monsters because I fink it's wrong even though I'm bigger than they are!"

Jagger and his mean friends thought this was very funny and they laughed and laughed. They were not going to leave Larry alone when they were having so much fun teasing him. Larry tried to ignore them, but soon began to realize that this wasn't the answer.

Finally, after he had listened to all he could take, he stood up and faced Jagger nose to nose. "Please leave me and the little monsters alone," he said firmly but politely. "Just because they are small and we are big, it isn't right to treat them any differently!"

This made Jagger very, very angry with Larry. He made a fist with his big, hairy hand and approached Larry with a threatening look on his face. "You better start picking on those small monsters or you'll be sorry!" Jagger demanded.

"Never," Larry replied. "I will never be mean to someone just because they're different. Just because you could...doesn't mean you should."

"You asked for it!" Jagger shouted. He raised his fist high and threw a punch in the direction of Larry, but Larry quickly moved out of the way and rolled on the ground. Instead of Larry, Jagger hit the large green rock that Larry had been sitting on and he let out a loud roar.

Jagger ran towards Larry, who was still lying on the ground. "Any last words?!" Jagger asked, and, again, he raised his fist and got ready to hit Larry.

But suddenly he stopped. The ground had started to rumble and everyone was scared...even Jagger.

They all looked at the large green rock. It was moving...and growing...and growling! And when it started to rise slowly out of the ground, they all realized at once that this wasn't a rock at all. It was a monster!

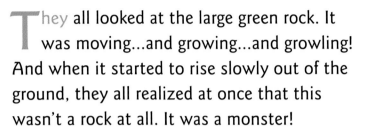

And it was a BIG monster! The biggest monster they had ever seen... bigger, by far, than any of the monsters in Monstoria! And not only was it big, it was mad!

"Who hit me while I was sleeping?" The giant monster demanded to know. All the other monsters looked at Jagger, and the giant monster quickly turned in Jagger's direction. His three yellow eyes focused on the mean, orange monster. Jagger, who was a big monster himself, seemed very small next to this giant.

"S-s-sorry!" Jagger said trembling. "I-I didn't know that you were a monster. I'm s-sorry!" The giant monster's face grew angrier. "GRRRR! This is for waking me up, you little orange hair ball!

Jagger was very scared and took off running. He ran as fast as he could, but the giant monster chased right behind him. "I'm so sorry!" pleaded Jagger. "I didn't mean to make you mad! I'm so sorry!"

They ran all around Monstoria. Through the trees, across the streams, and over the hills they went. The giant monster chased Jagger all the way to the mountains, where, finally, Jagger was cornered. There was no place left to run.

"I said I'm sorry!" Jagger cried. "It won't happen again...I promise!" It was no use. The giant monster showed his long claws and sharp teeth to frighten Jagger.

Jagger closed his eyes tightly and started to shake nervously.

Suddenly, off in the distance, someone cried "STOP!" in a very small, yet insistent, voice. The giant monster froze in his tracks and slowly turned his head in the direction of the plea.

It was Zabby! She stood there with a very worried look on her face and holding her toy in her arms. "Please don't hurt him!" Zabby pleaded. "I don't think he meant to wake you up. It was a mistake and I'm sure he's sorry."

Larry, finally catching up with the giant and Jagger, cautiously walked up and stood next to his friend, Zabby. The giant stared at the small blue monster and the big pink-striped monster being friendly to each other.

A large smile started to grow on the giant monster's face. "Well, I guess just because I could...doesn't mean I should," said the giant. Jagger looked very relieved as the giant stepped away from him.

"What's your name?" Larry asked the giant. "Viggo, my name is, Viggo," he answered with a smile. "Would you like a lollipop, Viggo?" Larry asked. "That would be nice, my small friend. Thank you," said the giant.

So for the first time in the land of Monstoria, all the monsters, big and small, furry and scaley, one-eyed, two-eyed or three, enjoyed each other's company while they ate their delicious lollipops. Larry the lollipop monster could not have been happier.

The End